Disclaimer

The information contained in this book is provided for educational and informational purposes only. It is not intended as, and should not be relied upon for, financial, investment, legal, or tax advice.

The authors of *123BTC: The Beginner's Guide to Bitcoin* are not licensed financial advisers. While every effort has been made to ensure the accuracy of the information presented, no guarantee is given that the content is complete, up to date, or suitable for your individual circumstances.

Readers are strongly encouraged to conduct their own research and seek independent professional advice from a qualified financial adviser, accountant, or legal professional before making any financial decisions.

The authors and publisher expressly disclaim any and all liability arising from actions taken, or not taken, based on the contents of this book. By reading this book, you acknowledge and agree that you are solely responsible for your own financial choices and outcomes.

How to Read This Book

This isn't a textbook or a crypto manual. It's a wake-up call.

What you'll read over the next twelve chapters is a story — one that begins with broken money and ends with a blueprint for freedom.

Here's how it flows:

- Chapters 1–5: expose the problem — how money was corrupted, inflated, and weaponised against everyday people.

- Chapters 6–8: reveal the solution — Bitcoin and the blockchain, explained simply, showing how technology can restore trust.

- Chapters 9–12: focus on you — how to protect your wealth, reclaim control, and prepare for what's coming next.

Each chapter builds on the one before it. So even if you've never owned a satoshi, start at the beginning — the story of *why* money broke is what makes understanding *how* Bitcoin fixes it so powerful.

By the time you reach the final page, you won't just understand Bitcoin. You'll understand money — and more importantly, the system that made it fail.

Contents

Introduction - What If Money is designed to fail?

You work hard. You save. You budget.
So why does it still feel like you're falling behind?

Your rent keeps going up.
Your groceries cost more every month.
Your savings grow slower than the prices around you.

It's not just "the economy." It's not just bad luck.
It's the system.
And it's working exactly as it was designed to.

Along with some help from my good friend Ardun Ward, I wrote this book because I've lived it too.
I'm not an economist. I'm not a tech bro.
Just an everyday person who started asking the question no one seemed to answer:

What if money itself is broken?

This book isn't about hype, or politics, or pushing an agenda.
It's about truth—made simple.
It's about helping you understand:

- **Why your dollars (or euros, or pesos) lose value every year.**

- **How central banks quietly rig the rules through inflation and debt.**

- **And why Bitcoin was created—not to make millionaires, but to give people a way out.**

You don't need a finance degree. You just need to understand what's happening—and what you can do about it. By the end of this book, you'll be able to:

- See **why the current system doesn't serve you!**

- Understand **how Bitcoin works in everyday terms!**

- Decide for yourself **whether it's time to take back control!**

Because the biggest risk today isn't investing in the wrong thing.

It's not knowing how the game is being played around you.

Let's fix that—together!

The Broken History of Money

Have you ever stopped and wondered—"why does it feel like no matter how hard I work, my money just doesn't go as far as it used to?"
You're not imagining it.
And it's not just "the economy." It's something deeper—something built into the very system of money itself.
This chapter isn't a history lesson for the sake of it.
It's a short walk through time to reveal one uncomfortable truth:
Money has been broken—again and again—for thousands of years.
And each time, it wasn't an accident.
It was tampered with, inflated, devalued... and ordinary people paid the price.

Let's go back to ancient Rome—an empire so powerful its roads are still walked on today. But even mighty Rome couldn't escape a problem that still haunts us now: broken money.
At first, Rome's currency was solid. The denarius, their silver coin, wasn't just symbolic—it held real, tangible value. It was made of nearly pure silver and trusted across a vast empire of over 60 million people. Soldiers were paid with it. Merchants traded with it. Ordinary citizens used it to buy their daily bread [1].
But running an empire is expensive—wars, armies, palaces, politics. And emperors didn't want to raise taxes. So, they found a shortcut: debase the currency.
Instead of finding more silver, they simply reduced how much silver was in each coin. The denarius that once held 100% silver quietly dropped to 90%, then 80%, then 50%. By the end, it was little more than a silver-coated copper disc [1].
At first, people didn't notice. But eventually, they did—especially when prices exploded.
What once cost 1 denarius suddenly cost 2... then 10... then 100. A loaf of bread that used to be affordable now required 200 coins. Why?
Because the money was no longer real. As the silver vanished, so did

trust. Merchants demanded more coins to make up for what was lost. People stopped using the coins. They hoarded goods, returned to bartering, and did everything they could to escape a money system that no longer worked [1].

Sound familiar?

Now let's move east to ancient China, where a similar story played out—this time not with silver, but paper.

Around 1000 AD, during the Song Dynasty, China became the first civilization to use government-backed paper money. It was revolutionary. Instead of mining metal, the government could now simply print value into existence [2].

And at first, it worked. Trade flourished. The economy soared. Paper money made commerce faster and lighter. But the same temptation crept in easy money.

Later dynasties—especially under Kublai Khan and the Yuan—abused the system. To fund wars and massive infrastructure projects, they flooded the economy with paper notes, unbacked by anything tangible [2].

The result? Collapse.

Prices surged. Daily essentials like rice, silk, and salt became unaffordable. Why? Because the supply of money ballooned, while the supply of goods stayed the same. More money was chasing the same amount of stuff, making everything more expensive.

As confidence crumbled, people stopped trusting the paper. They hoarded silver. They returned to bartering. The promise of paper was broken—and trust, once lost, didn't return [2].

Fast forward to the 1500s, and we arrive in Spain, a country that stumbled into extraordinary wealth.

After discovering vast silver mines in the Americas—especially Cerro Rico in Bolivia—Spain flooded Europe with silver.

At first, it felt like an economic miracle. But just like with Rome and China, too much easy money became a poison. Prices across Europe tripled over the next century. The value of silver plummeted. Spain's economy, once booming, began to collapse under the weight of inflation and debt [3].

Then there's France, in the early 1700s.
Facing national bankruptcy, France handed over its financial system to a Scottish economist named John Law. His solution? A central bank that issued paper money, backed by shares in a colonial trading company [4]. It worked brilliantly—until it didn't.
The money supply ballooned. The shares became worthless. Inflation exploded. The entire system collapsed within a few years, and Law fled the country in disgrace [4].

In the 20th century, things didn't improve much. The tools became more sophisticated, but the pattern stayed the same.
In Germany after World War I, the government printed massive amounts of money to pay off war debts. The result? Hyperinflation so extreme that people used wheelbarrows of cash to buy bread. In 1923, a single U.S. dollar was worth over 4 trillion German marks. A lifetime of savings became worthless overnight [5].
Zimbabwe repeated the disaster in the early 2000s. To fund government spending and cover collapsing industries, they printed money non-stop. Inflation peaked at 79.6 billion percent per month. People were bringing suitcases of money to the store—just to buy a loaf of bread [6].

And in Venezuela, in the 2010s, oil prices collapsed, and the government printed money to fill the gap. Inflation soared above 1 million percent. Families who once lived comfortably found themselves unable to buy basic food [7].

Each time, it's the same pattern:

1. A currency starts out trusted and sound.

2. Then it's slowly or suddenly debased—either by removing precious metals or printing more than is sustainable.

3. Eventually, people lose trust, inflation explodes, and the economy falls into chaos.
Different countries. Different centuries. Same result.

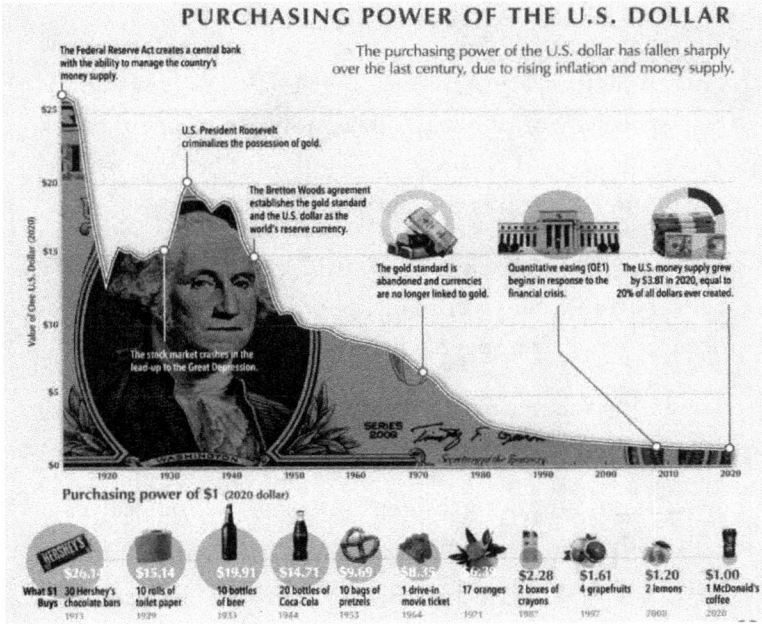

PURCHASING POWER OF THE U.S. DOLLAR

The purchasing power of the U.S. dollar has fallen sharply over the last century, due to rising inflation and money supply.

The Federal Reserve Act creates a central bank with the ability to manage the country's money supply.

U.S. President Roosevelt criminalizes the possession of gold.

The Bretton Woods agreement establishes the gold standard and the U.S. dollar as the world's reserve currency.

The gold standard is abandoned and currencies are no longer linked to gold.

Quantitative easing (QE1) begins in response to the financial crisis.

The U.S. money supply grew by $3.8T in 2020, equal to 20% of all dollars ever created.

The stock market crashes in the lead-up to the Great Depression.

Value of One U.S. Dollar (2020)

Purchasing power of $1 (2020 dollar)

What $1 Buys	30 Hershey's chocolate bars	10 rolls of toilet paper	10 bottles of beer	20 bottles of Coca-Cola	10 bags of pretzels	1 drive-in movie ticket	17 oranges	2 boxes of crayons	4 grapefruits	2 lemons	1 McDonald's coffee
	$26.14	$15.14	$19.91	$14.71	$9.69	$8.35		$2.28	$1.61	$1.20	$1.00
	1913	1929	1933	1944	1953	1964	1971	1987	1997	2008	2020

Inflated Fiat: Your Purchasing Power is Shrinking

Why does this keep happening?
Because when governments control money, they're always tempted to create more of it—especially during wars, recessions, or political crises. But when new money is created without adding new goods or productivity to match it, inflation is the result.

And without something real to back it—like gold, or a fixed supply—it's almost guaranteed to be abused. Eventually, people lose faith. Businesses stop trusting prices. Savings disappear. The economy breaks down.

It's not just bad luck. It's the natural consequence of money being unlimited—and centrally controlled.

In 1971, the United States—under President Nixon—cut the dollar's final tie to gold. Until then, a U.S. dollar could, in theory, be exchanged for real gold. It gave the currency discipline, and it gave people confidence in its value [8].

But once that link was severed, dollars could be printed at will. And they were.

Since then, the U.S. dollar has lost over 90% of its purchasing power. In simple terms, what cost $1 in 1970 now costs over $8. That same dollar in your wallet stretches less and less every year [9].

This isn't just a U.S. problem. Australia, Europe, Canada—it's the same story. Money has become unlimited, unbacked, and deeply unstable.

And while central banks and politicians say it's all under control—your grocery bill, rent, and savings account say otherwise.

That's the pattern. The faces and flags change. But the system doesn't.

When money is easy to create, its value becomes easy to destroy. And the people at the top—whether emperors or economists—rarely feel the fallout. Why? Because those closest to the money printer benefit first, using the new money to buy tangible assets like real estate, stocks, and land—before the rest of society realises prices have gone up.

So, who feels the pain? The common person on the street who doesn't understand what is taking place. If it feels like we're heading for a breaking point again… it's because we are.

In the next chapter, we'll show you how today's money—fiat currency— is built to lose value from the start. Not by mistake, but by design.

It's time to understand what you're holding in your hands—and why it's quietly losing its power.

The cash in your hand feels real—until it starts melting away.

Each week, you feel it. Groceries are up. Rent is worse. A takeaway meal that once cost $20 now costs $35. Your wage might have nudged up, but it's not keeping pace with the increasing everyday costs. If you're not already using a credit card to plug the gap, you probably know someone who is.

This isn't "just the economy."
It's inflation—and it's not a glitch in the system. It is the system itself.

If that sounds bad enough on paper, it's even worse in the digital age— because today's money isn't just printed, it's conjured.

Paper Promises and Digital Magic

Last chapter, we explored how fiat currencies throughout history—like those of ancient Rome, revolutionary France, and post-war Germany— collapsed under the weight of their own manipulation. Coins were clipped, paper was printed, value dissolved.

Modern fiat currencies haven't escaped the same fate—they've just digitized the downfall.

Today's money isn't even printed anymore—it's conjured from nothing. Central banks create it with a few keystrokes. Trillions can appear overnight, like they did during COVID bailouts and stimulus waves [10]. The number of dollars goes up. But what you can buy with them? That goes down.

Fiat currencies—your dollars, euros, pesos, naira—aren't backed by gold, oil, or anything real. They're backed by belief. Governments declare the value, and you're expected to accept it. That's the deal.

But here's the catch:
They can create more with a keystroke.
You, the worker, the saver, the citizen—can't.
And in that imbalance, power wins and people lose.

The Hidden Tax That Touches Everyone

When a government floods the economy with new money, it doesn't magically create more food, homes, or fuel. It just dilutes the value of what already exists.

This is inflation.

Your money buys less because there's more of it out there.

The result is felt globally, but it hits hardest for those without assets—people who don't own homes or stocks, who save in cash and live pay check to pay check.

From Turkey to Venezuela, inflation has crushed currencies, forcing families to carry wheelbarrows of cash or storm banks for their savings [7].

This isn't happening in the distant past. It's happening now.

Even in so-called "stable" economies, it's getting harder to ignore. The U.S. printed over 40% of all existing dollars between 2020 and 2022 alone [11]. Australia's Reserve Bank admitted it misread the inflation surge and raised interest rates too late [12]. The UK's pound suffered its worst collapse in decades [13].

Globally, people are waking up to the same quiet truth:
Their money isn't protecting them. It's betraying them.

The Everyday Impact
Let's break this down in real-world terms.
Say you're a factory worker in the Philippines earning ₱20,000 a month. Your rice, oil, and fuel all rise in cost by 20% in a year. But your wage increase? Just 5%.
That gap isn't theoretical. It's the difference between sending your kids to school or not. Between paying your power bill or letting it lapse.
Or imagine a young couple in London trying to save for a home. Each year, house prices rise faster than their savings. What felt like a 3-year goal becomes 5. Then 10. Then "maybe never."
You're not lazy. You're not bad with money.
The system is quietly devaluing your time and effort.
Inflation is theft—but dressed in an invisible cape.

Why the System Likes It This Way
You might be wondering: if inflation hurts so many people, why let it happen?
Simple. It benefits those in power.
Governments can "pay off" their debts with devalued money. Central banks manipulate interest rates and print money to avoid accountability. Businesses raise prices to stay ahead. And financial institutions—who lend money—benefit when that money is repaid in weaker currency.
Inflation is an invisible tax. And it's one you never voted for.
As economist Saifedean Ammous put it, inflation lets governments tax people without legislation, permission, or protest [14].
And when things spiral, like in Argentina or Zimbabwe, those who saw it early flee into U.S. dollars or gold—if they can.

But what happens when even the dollar starts to slide?
What happens when there's nowhere else to run?

The Illusion of Growth

They'll tell you the economy is growing. GDP is up. Markets are up. Spending is up.

But are you up?

If your pay increased 3%, but inflation was 7%, you got a 4% pay cut in disguise. If you saved $10,000 and it now buys $9,200 worth of goods, that's not growth—it's erosion.

When the economy "grows" by printing more money, it's like measuring wealth with a rubber ruler. It stretches. But nothing real has changed.

That's why billionaires get richer—because they hold assets like stocks, land, and equity. And you're left holding cash, which shrinks in real time.

The Slow Boil

In 1971, a home in the U.S. cost around $25,000. Today? It's closer to $400,000 [15].

Did the home change that much? Or did the money?

They say inflation averages 2%–3% per year. But that's like saying a leaking boat only takes on a few drops per minute. You still sink—just more slowly.

Over a decade, 3% inflation compounds to nearly 30% loss in value.

In 20 years? You've lost almost half your purchasing power.

Like a frog in slowly heated water, you don't notice—until you're cooked.

The Wake-Up Call

Here's the bottom line:

If you save in fiat, you're guaranteed to lose.

If you work for fiat, your time is being devalued.

If you believe governments will reverse this trend, history says otherwise.

This isn't about panic. It's about understanding.

It's about awareness. So, you can act before it's too late.

Because inflation isn't just about prices.

It's about control.

And once you see how this system is wired, you'll understand why Bitcoin was built—not to make you rich overnight, but to give you an honest alternative.

But before we get there, we need to understand who really controls your currency—and why they don't want you asking these questions.

Centralised vs Decentralised Currency

In moments of crisis, money tells the truth.

When economies fall apart, when trust disappears, when governments panic—the structure behind a currency becomes exposed. And in country after country, from different continents, eras, and political systems, we see a repeating pattern: when the money is controlled by a central authority, the people pay the price.

Let's look at what this really means—not through theory, but through real events that hit real families.

AR **Argentina, December 2001**

In late 2001, Argentina's economy collapsed under the weight of unsustainable debt, corruption, and currency mismanagement. In response, the government froze all bank accounts and restricted cash withdrawals. You could only access a small portion of your own savings—if anything at all. ATMs were locked. People lined up in panic, banging on the steel doors of banks that no longer served them.

A butcher who had worked for decades found his life savings—50,000 pesos—suddenly worth a fraction of what they were a month earlier. Once enough to support him for a year, now it barely covered a week's worth of meat [16].

Protests erupted. Tires burned in the streets. Shops were looted. Their money hadn't just lost value—it had been taken from them by decree.

GR **Greece, 2015**

In the heart of the European Union, Greece faced a debt crisis so severe that banks shut their doors and ATMs were capped at just €60 per withdrawal [17]. Pensioners queued in the summer heat, desperate to access their retirement funds. Businesses couldn't pay for imports. Families resorted to bartering—trading olives and wine for basic goods.

On paper, their savings still existed. But centralized control meant they couldn't touch it. Their money was locked away, and there was nothing they could do.

VE Venezuela, 2016–2019

Venezuela experienced one of the worst hyperinflation crises in modern history. Prices doubled every few days. Salaries became meaningless. It got so bad that stacks of cash were used to make handbags or wallpaper, because they were worth less than the materials themselves.

People began trading in U.S. dollars, bartering food, or turning to digital alternatives. Bitcoin adoption rose as a lifeline—not for speculation, but for survival. It allowed Venezuelans to receive money from abroad, store value safely, and escape the government's broken currency [7].

LB Lebanon, 2019–2021

When Lebanon's banking system collapsed, withdrawals were restricted to just a few hundred dollars a month—no matter how much you had deposited. Salaries disappeared. Parents couldn't pay school fees.

People stormed their own banks to demand their savings, often being arrested in the process.

Trust in the financial system didn't just erode—it imploded. With no alternative, families were forced to barter, beg, or rely on relatives abroad sending money through underground channels.

CA Canada, 2022

In Canada 2022, a mechanic's savings were frozen without warning for donating to a protest, showing even 'stable' systems can seize control [11].

Even if you disagreed with the protest itself, the message was chilling: your money is not truly yours if someone else holds the keys.

TR **Turkey, 2023**

Turkey was hit by a massive inflation wave after years of reckless central bank policy. By 2023, official inflation soared past 80% [18]—and even that was likely understated.

Bread prices doubled. Fuel became unaffordable. $500 million in trade stalled as trust in the lira collapsed.

Those closest to the ruling class escaped early, converting their wealth into dollars and euros. Everyone else paid the price, watching their wages evaporate week by week.

🔓 One Pattern, Many Countries

From South America to Europe, from authoritarian regimes to democracies, the same pattern emerges again and again:
• Crisis hits.
• The government tightens control.
• Banks limit access.
• Inflation robs the value of savings.
• And people suffer—while those in power escape unharmed.
The core problem isn't the country. It's the structure.
Fiat currency is centralized. That means:
• It can be printed or frozen at will.
• It's held in banks you don't control.
• Its value depends entirely on trust in politicians, bureaucrats, and central bankers.
And when that trust breaks? The whole system starts to shake.
Now imagine this: you wake up to find your grocery bill has tripled. That alone is stressful. But then you head to the bank to withdraw money—just enough to feed your family—and you're told you can't access your own savings. No explanation. No exception. Just a locked door and a

frozen account.

This isn't fiction. It's reality for millions. And if it hasn't happened to you yet, that doesn't mean it won't.

Because when money is centralized, control isn't yours—it's theirs.

🔓 What If There's Another Way?

Imagine a currency that:

- No government can freeze.
- No central bank can inflate.
- No single entity can manipulate or control.
- One you can send to anyone, anywhere, anytime—without permission.

That's what decentralized currency offers.

Bitcoin, for example, has a fixed supply—21 million units, ever. It doesn't inflate. It isn't issued by a state. It's secured by a global network of computers. Transactions are transparent, irreversible, and verified by consensus—not command.

Where fiat bends to politics, Bitcoin follows math.

Where banks require permission, Bitcoin needs only a connection.

Where fiat savings can evaporate overnight, Bitcoin stands outside that system entirely.

Unlike centralized money, decentralized money is built for the people— not for those who wish to control them.

🛠 The Future Is Being Built

In 2009, a quiet piece of open-source code began circulating online. It came with no promises, no hype—just a question:

"What if we didn't need to trust the powerful anymore?"

That code became Bitcoin.

And from Cyprus to Argentina, Lebanon to Canada, people are beginning to answer that question—not in theory, but in action.

Some use it to escape the grip of inflation.

Some to protect their privacy.

Some to send money across borders when banks shut the doors. But all of them are using it for the same reason: freedom. Decentralized money gives people back control.

It lets you save, spend, and send your wealth—on your terms. No gatekeepers. No approvals. No frozen accounts. Just you, using your money how you want, when you want, where you want.

It's not just about avoiding collapse—it's about reclaiming power. Because when centralized money fails, decentralized money doesn't just step in—it hands the freedom back to the people.

FRANKIE BOYLE
'Bankers are looting the world. You're not in the middle of a recession; you're in the middle of robbery.'

QE and QT: The Money Pump and Squeeze

You hear it on the news—quantitative easing, quantitative tightening, liquidity injections, balance sheet normalization. Fancy terms designed to sound complicated, even untouchable.

But here's the truth: they use big words to keep you confused, to stop you asking the hard questions.

Strip away the jargon, and it's really just a simple game: turn the money tap on—or slam it shut—and watch what happens to your wallet.

Prices rise. Wages don't. Loans get tighter. Life gets harder.

Let's unpack how this works—and why it matters to you.

The Big Flood: What QE Really Means

Imagine money like soup in a big pot. You've got just enough for four bowls. Now the government opens a faucet and pours in more water to stretch it further. More people get soup—but it's thinner, weaker, and doesn't fill you up the same. That's quantitative easing.

The government or central bank doesn't literally print cash. They push a button. And just like that, trillions of digital dollars appear [19].

They use that money to buy bonds and assets, which drives interest rates down and floods the financial system with liquidity. On paper, it sounds helpful. But the money doesn't flow into your pocket.

It flows into banks, hedge funds, and corporations. And you're left watching everything around you get more expensive.

QE in Action: 2008 and the $12 Trillion Band-Aid

In 2008, when Lehman Brothers collapsed and banks started failing, the

U.S. Federal Reserve began pumping out money fast. Over the next few years, central banks around the world created roughly $12 trillion to keep the system from falling apart [19].

Banks got bailouts. Corporations got lifelines. And yes, some jobs were saved. But here's what *you* felt:
- Gas prices jumped from $3 to $5 a gallon [20].
- Used cars climbed from $10,000 to $13,000 [21].
- Groceries soared—barbecue ribs suddenly cost 20% more [22].

Did you get a bonus? A pay raise? A break?
No—you got the bill.

2020: Same Playbook, Different Crisis

When COVID hit, the world froze. Lockdowns, layoffs, shuttered stores. The U.S. responded with another $4 trillion—part of a global $10 trillion QE wave [19].

You might've received a stimulus check—$1,200, maybe $2,000 [10]. But that check didn't stretch far when:
- Eggs jumped from $2 to $4.
- Gas hit $50 a tank.
- Lumber for your porch doubled to $1,000 [24].

It was like ordering one pizza for the table. Then ten extra people showed up—and no new pizza was ordered. Each slice got smaller.

Between 2020 and 2023, consumer prices rose more than 15%, while wages climbed just 5% [25]. Your dollar didn't stretch. It shrank.

PURCHASING POWER
SINCE 2020

+1,200%   − 25%

QE: The Silent Tax

Governments love QE because it hides the cost of bad decisions. Don't want to raise taxes? Just "print" the money. Need to save the stock market? Hit the liquidity switch.

But nothing is free. You pay for it at the checkout line.

- A latte that cost $2.50 now costs $4 [26].
- Rent that was $1,000 is now $1,150 [27].
- Soccer boots for your kid jumped from $70 to $100 [28].

Half the world survives on $5 a day. In some places, $5 once bought a meal. Now it buys a snack [29].

And while your grocery bill climbs, the bankers who caused the crash are celebrating record bonuses.

QT: The Squeeze

So what happens when all that easy money overheats the economy? Enter Quantitative Tightening—QT. The faucet gets shut off. Money is pulled back. Interest rates rise. Borrowing slows. And the economy— already groaning—starts gasping for breath.

In 2022, with inflation spiking to 9% in the U.S. and 10% in Europe [9], central banks slammed the brakes. The Fed hiked rates from near zero to over 5% in under a year [30].

Mortgage payments ballooned. A $300,000 home that cost $1,200/month in 2021 now costs $1,700/month [31].

Business loans dried up. Credit cards got nastier. Your cousin's café? Gone—shut down after she couldn't secure funding [32].

Here's the kicker: QT doesn't bring prices back down. It just makes life harder.

Groceries stayed high. Utility bills climbed. Job openings shrank. And your raise? Probably never came.

Flood, Squeeze, Repeat

Since 2008, central banks have pumped more than $20 trillion into the global economy [19].

It didn't fix the system. It built a treadmill:
• QE: Create money → inflate everything → pretend it's fine
• QT: Hike rates → crash spending → act surprised when people can't cope

In the U.S., government debt has exploded—from $10 trillion in 2008 to over $33 trillion today, climbing by $1 trillion every 100 days [20].

Prices soared. Wages didn't. Savings eroded.
People ran faster but got nowhere.

And now, it's personal.

You do everything right—work hard, save what you can, cut back where it hurts. Yet the rent goes up. The groceries shrink. The bills pile higher.

It's not just exhausting. It's engineered that way.

Because this system doesn't want you ahead.
It wants you dependent.

This Isn't a Bug. It's Fiat.
QE and QT are just tools in a deeper game. The real issue? Fiat money has no anchor.
There's no gold. No cap. Just keystrokes and policy.
Governments spend what they want and print what they can't collect.
Central banks juggle interest rates and bond sales like carnival tricks. And every time they get it wrong—you get hit.
Rent. Food. Fuel. Insurance. It's all rising. And your bank balance is getting smaller.

It's Not Just Numbers—It's You
Your barbecue costs $15 a pound now, not $10 [22]. Your electricity bill is up 20% [20]. "You're forced to decide whether to drive to work or put food on the table."
Canada's gas hit $6/gallon in 2022 [13]. Australia's burgers jumped from $8 to $12 [21]. Half the world can't afford lunch.
As fiat's $310 trillion debt buries economies, everyday costs—like food, fuel, and rent—outpace your paycheck, pushing families to the edge and demanding a new solution [20].

So, What Happens When the Faucet Breaks?
History leaves us clues.
Germany in the 1920s. Argentina in the 1980s. Japan in the 1990s.
All pumped, all squeezed—until their economies finally buckled [5], [16], [33].

Today it's subtler. But the cracks are there. And you feel them.

QE didn't save you. QT won't fix it.
Because fiat money was never built for you.
It was built to serve power.

And this pump-and-squeeze cycle?
It's not just broken.
It's breaking.

Next, we'll look at what's happening right now in the fiat world—and why, if you don't act soon, you could be caught in the collapse before you even know it's here.

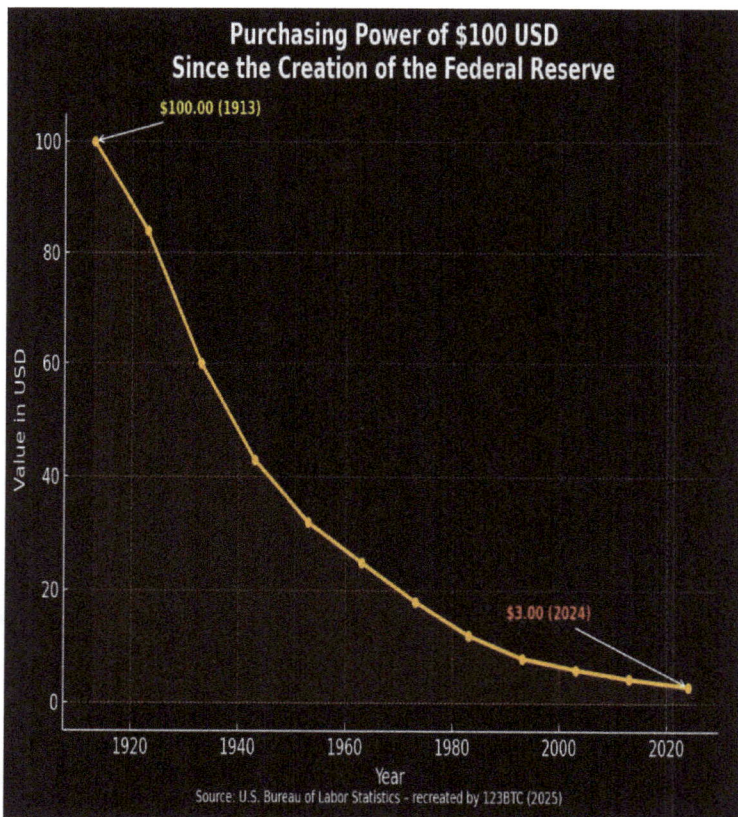

Purchasing Power of $100 USD Since the Creation of the Federal Reserve

$100.00 (1913)

$3.00 (2024)

Value in USD

Year

Source: U.S. Bureau of Labor Statistics - recreated by 123BTC (2025)

The Breaking Point — Fiat's Global Implosion

The Money Printing Madness

Since the 2008 financial crisis, governments and central banks have flooded the world with more than $30 trillion of new money — an amount larger than the combined GDP of the U.S., China, and Japan [19].

This isn't just a number on a screen. It's a tidal wave of cash created out of thin air — meant to prop up failing banks, bail out corporations, and "stimulate" economies that were already broken.

To put this in perspective:

- From 1960 to 2008 — nearly five decades — the U.S. Federal Reserve expanded its balance sheet slowly and cautiously.

- From 2008 to 2023 — just fifteen years — that balance sheet exploded from about $900 billion to over $9 trillion. A tenfold increase [30].

Globally, central banks created more money in this short period than in all previous decades combined. The result of all this? Fiat currencies around the world are losing their grip.

Fiat's Global Collapse

Inflation isn't just rising — it's spiralling out of control.

- In Europe, energy prices doubled in a matter of months in 2022, pushing millions into fuel poverty [34].

- In Argentina, the peso crashed repeatedly, triggering bank freezes and sparking civil unrest [35].

- In Sri Lanka, years of debt mismanagement and currency failure ended in 2022 with food shortages, fuel queues, and political upheaval [36].

From Lebanon's frozen savings to Venezuela's collapsing bolivar, the pattern is the same: when money can be created without limit, trust eventually disappears — and with it, stability.

The Time Bomb of Debt

Beneath it all lies a deeper crisis: the world is drowning in debt.

Global debt has soared to $310 trillion — three times the planet's annual economic output [20].

This isn't just a number. It's a time bomb.

Every year, governments owe billions in interest alone. But they don't have the money saved. So they borrow more to cover the old debts — adding fresh interest with every round.

It's a treadmill: borrow → pay interest → borrow again.

Paying it down would mean raising taxes or slashing spending — political suicide. Defaulting would trigger global chaos. So governments take the "easy" way out: print more money.

But that fuels inflation and quietly erodes your savings.

In the U.S. alone, $850 billion is now spent annually just servicing debt — more than the yearly budgets of most nations [37].

The Human Cost

And as always, it's ordinary people who carry the burden.

- Rents climb higher.

- Savings lose value.

- Food, fuel, and medicine get harder to afford.

Half the world lives on less than $5 a day — and those dollars buy less every year [29].

Maybe you've skipped a meal to stretch your budget. Delayed a doctor's visit. Put off repairing the car. Not because you're careless — but because the system quietly steals from you every time money is printed.

Even when wages rise, they rarely keep pace. A 3% raise feels meaningless when prices jump 7%. That's not a raise — it's a pay cut in disguise.

This is the invisible tax of fiat. You don't see it deducted on a payslip, but you feel it every time you shop, pay rent, or fill the tank.

Cracks in the System

The cracks are no longer subtle.

- Trust in banks is at historic lows [38].
- Savings accounts pay next to nothing while inflation eats away balances in real time.
- Protests over inequality are erupting worldwide.

This isn't some distant or abstract threat. It's here. It's now.

And history shows what happens when fiat systems collapse:

- Economies seize up.
- Food disappears from shelves.
- Jobs vanish.
- Streets erupt in unrest.
- Families lose their savings overnight.

This isn't theory. It's happened again and again.

The Breaking Point

So, the question is no longer *if* fiat fails.

It's *when*. And how badly.

At this breaking point, we need something different. A way to store and send value that doesn't depend on printing presses, mountains of debt, or the promises of politicians.

A system built not to trap you — but to set you free.

Up to now, this book has focused on the people — those who've suffered under the failures of centralised money. But to truly understand the solution, we need to look under the hood of how Bitcoin works.

From here, my good friend, Ardun Ward, takes the lead. His voice carries a deeper technical rhythm — one born of years studying Bitcoin's code, network, and purpose.

You'll feel a change in tone, but the mission remains the same: to help you see that freedom in money isn't a dream — it's already being built.

Bitcoin — A New Foundation

This is where the story turns. After centuries of broken promises, something new was born — not in a government lab, but in the mind of an anonymous coder who wanted to give power back to the people.

The system is crumbling. The dollar is losing its grip, global trust in fiat money has fallen to just 18% [38], and a $310 trillion debt monster looms over everything [20]. By now, you can feel it: the ground shifting beneath your financial feet. Fiat money isn't just flawed—it's on life support, wobbling like a three-legged table held together by blind faith and printed promises. But what if someone saw this collapse coming—and built something better? Not a patch. Not a tweak. But an entirely new foundation. A table that no government, no banker, no bureaucrat could flip.

That spark came in 2008, just as the world was spiralling into a financial meltdown. Banks collapsed. Bailouts poured in. The system gasped under the weight of its own leverage and lies [19].

Out of that chaos, a quiet message appeared on a cryptography mailing list. A white paper. A solution.

Bitcoin.

This wasn't just another digital currency. This was money that couldn't be printed on a whim. It was a set of rules—without rulers. It was built to outlast the manipulators who broke the last system [39].

So now that we've seen what fiat really is—bloated, corruptible, dying— let's explore what Bitcoin is and why it matters.

```
              Bitcoin Genesis Block
                   Raw Hex Version

00000000   01 00 00 00 00 00 00 00   00 00 00 00 00 00 00 00   ................
00000010   00 00 00 00 00 00 00 00   00 00 00 00 00 00 00 00   ................
00000020   00 00 00 00 3B A3 ED FD   7A 7B 12 B2 7A C7 2C 3E   ....;£íý z{.²zÇ,>
00000030   67 76 8F 61 7F C8 1B C3   88 8A 51 32 3A 9F B8 AA   gv.a.È.Ã.ŠQ2:Ÿ.ª
00000040   4B 1E 5E 4A 29 AB 5F 49   FF FF 00 1D 1D AC 2B 7C   K.^J)«_Iÿÿ...¬+|
00000050   01 01 00 00 00 01 00 00   00 00 00 00 00 00 00 00   ................
00000060   00 00 00 00 00 00 00 00   00 00 00 00 00 00 00 00   ................
00000070   00 00 00 00 00 00 FF FF   FF FF 4D 04 FF FF 00 1D   ......ÿÿÿÿM.ÿÿ..
00000080   01 04 45 54 68 65 20 54   69 6D 65 73 20 30 33 2F   ..EThe Times 03/
00000090   4A 61 6E 2F 32 30 30 39   20 43 68 61 6E 63 65 6C   Jan/2009 Chancel
000000A0   6C 6F 72 20 6F 6E 20 62   72 69 6E 6B 20 6F 66 20   lor on brink of
000000B0   73 65 63 6F 6E 64 20 62   61 69 6C 6F 75 74 20 66   second bailout f
000000C0   6F 72 20 62 61 6E 6B 73   FF FF FF FF 01 00 F2 05   or banksÿÿÿÿ..ò.
000000D0   2A 01 00 00 00 43 41 04   67 8A FD B0 FE 55 48 27   *....CA.gŠý°þUH'
000000E0   19 67 F1 A6 71 30 B7 10   5C D6 A8 28 E0 39 09 A6   .gñ¦q0·.\Ö¨(à9.¦
000000F0   79 62 E0 EA 1F 61 DE B6   49 F6 BC 3F 4C EF 38 C4   ybàê.aÞ¶Iö¼?Lï8Ä
00000100   F3 55 04 E5 1E C1 12 DE   5C 38 4D F7 BA 0B 8D 57   óU.å.Á.Þ\8M÷º..W
00000110   8A 4C 70 2B 6B F1 1D 5F   AC 00 00 00 00            ŠLp+kñ._¬....
```

Bitcoin: Hard Money for a Soft World

Bitcoin is a decentralised digital currency with a hard-coded supply cap: there will only ever be 21 million coins [39]. This isn't a promise from a politician—it's code. Open source. Public. Immutable [40].

New bitcoins aren't created out of thin air. They're earned by miners who run powerful computers to secure the network. Every 10 minutes, these miners compete to solve complex cryptographic puzzles. The winner earns newly minted bitcoin and the right to validate the next block of transactions [41].

This process—called proof-of-work—isn't free. It consumes real-world electricity. That cost is a feature, not a bug. It makes cheating expensive and honesty profitable. You can't fake the work. You can't print rewards. You must earn them [42].

This is where the term "blockchain" comes in. Each new group of transactions is a "block." Every block links to the one before it, forming a secure, transparent chain of verified data—public for all, but unchangeable by any one party [39].

The blockchain contains every transaction since Bitcoin's birth. These blocks are added every 10 minutes, stacked like layers of digital truth. They are visible to anyone via explorers like mempool.space and locked in forever [43]. Bitcoin acts as a global ledger—permanent, public, and incorruptible [40].

It's also incredibly reliable. Since the genesis block was mined by Satoshi Nakamoto on January 3, 2009, the network has enjoyed 99.999% uptime [44]. Compare that to banks that close on weekends, crash during crises, or fall victim to cyberattacks. Bitcoin doesn't close. It doesn't pause. It doesn't break.

The Halving: Built-In Scarcity

Bitcoin's supply schedule is just as radical. Every 210,000 blocks (roughly every 4 years), the amount of new bitcoin entering circulation gets cut in half—a process known as the halving [41].

At launch, miners earned 50 BTC per block. After the first halving, it became 25 BTC, then 12.5 BTC, and now it's 3.125 BTC [41]. This continues until the final bitcoin is mined sometime around the year 2140 [40].

That's the opposite of fiat money, which expands until it collapses or resets. Bitcoin is deflationary. It grows scarcer. And it rewards early adopters—especially miners who secured the network when rewards were higher [39].

This structure flips the fiat model on its head. In today's system, those closest to the money printer—governments, banks, insiders—get rich first. Everyone else gets leftovers. In Bitcoin, everyone plays by the same rules. No one gets special access. No one gets bailed out.

Bitcoin is money for the people. Global. Permissionless. Predictable. It doesn't care where you were born or how much influence you have. That's its power—and the reason we had to break down fiat before introducing it.

But What Happens When All Bitcoin Is Mined?

Good question. Even after the last bitcoin is mined, miners will still be incentivised. Why? Because in addition to the block reward, miners also collect transaction fees [39].

As adoption grows, these fees will be enough to justify securing the network [40]. Just like Uber drivers earn from rides, not tips alone, future miners will profit from processing transactions. If Bitcoin is widely used—and all signs point that way—the network will be self-sustaining.

Energy and the Real World

Bitcoin doesn't just live in cyberspace. It's rooted in the physical world. Unlike fiat, which is printed at zero cost and infinite scale, Bitcoin's creation demands energy—watts of real electricity [42].

This is often attacked. In 2023, Greenpeace launched the "Skull of Satoshi," a campaign smearing Bitcoin's energy use [45]. Ironically, Bitcoiners adopted the skull as a badge of honour.

But here's the truth: Bitcoin's energy use isn't wasteful—it's foundational [42]. Because miners are profit-driven, they hunt for the cheapest energy. Often that means stranded power, like gas flaring or unused hydropower [46]. Bitcoin turns waste into wealth and could even lead to new innovations in global energy distribution.

Bitcoin Is a Protocol, not a tech company

Bitcoin isn't a company. It's not a startup. It's a protocol—like the internet [39].

Just as the internet runs on layers (Ethernet, TCP/IP, HTTP), Bitcoin combines cryptography (SHA-256), GPS timestamping, and other technologies into a cohesive system. Protocols are powerful because they don't need permission. They're adopted, not sold [47].

Some critics say Bitcoin is too slow. They compare it to faster blockchains like Solana or XRP. But this misunderstands Bitcoin's priorities [48].

Bitcoin was designed to prioritise decentralisation and security over raw speed. That's the Blockchain Trilemma: you can have two of the following—security, decentralisation, scalability—but not all three [49]. Satoshi chose wisely.

That's where Layer 2 solutions like the Lightning Network come in. They enable fast, cheap payments without bloating the main chain [50]. Think of it like running a tab at a bar, then settling up all at once.

Satoshi's: The Smallest Unit of Bitcoin

What about divisibility? If Bitcoin is worth $100,000 someday, how do you buy a coffee?

Each bitcoin is divisible into 100 million Satoshi's. That means there are 2.1 quadrillion units to go around [40]. In the future, you might not say "this costs 0.0002 BTC"—you'll say, "this coffee is 2,000 sats." Just like we price houses in millions and gum in cents.

You Don't Have To
Buy 1 Bitcoin

A satoshi is the smallest unit of bitcoin, equivalent to 0.00000001 btc

1 Satoshi	= 0.0000000**1** BTC
10 Satoshi	= 0.000000**10** BTC
100 Satoshi	= 0.00000**100** BTC
1,000 Satoshi	= 0.0000**1000** BTC
10,000 Satoshi	= 0.000**10000** BTC
100,000 Satoshi	= 0.00**100000** BTC
1m Satoshi	= 0.0**1000000** BTC
10m Satoshi	= 0.**10000000** BTC
100m Satoshi	= **1**.00000000 BTC

The Digital Doesn't Mean Fake

Some people say Bitcoin isn't real because you can't hold it.

But ask yourself: when was the last time you held the numbers in your bank account? The digital revolution is already here—we just haven't fully noticed. From water plants to stock markets, most of our world runs on digital systems [51].

The difference? Bitcoin is backed by something tangible: energy. You can't create it without expending electricity. That makes it real in a way fiat can never be [42].

What If the Internet Goes Down?

Another concern: if Bitcoin is digital, what happens during an outage? Enter the nodes. These are lightweight computers that store and validate the blockchain. They're distributed globally—anyone can run one. There are over 60,000 nodes worldwide, many operating on small laptops or Raspberry Pi devices [52].

If the internet fails in one region, Bitcoin keeps going. Even a global outage wouldn't kill it—because once the internet returns, nodes sync back up. No downtime. No loss. Just resilience [40].

Unlike centralised systems that crash under pressure, Bitcoin survives through distribution. It has no head to cut off. No weak point to exploit.

Bitcoin isn't perfect. But in a collapsing financial world, it's the best foundation we've ever had. Immutable. Transparent. Fair.

In the next chapter, we'll unpack the technology that makes it all possible—and why the blockchain is about much more than just money.

What Is the Blockchain?

Last chapter, we explored Bitcoin: a monetary system built on fairness, scarcity, and decentralisation. But what makes it all work beneath the surface? What gives it the power to resist manipulation, censorship, or collapse?

The answer is the blockchain.

Often used as a buzzword, the blockchain is far more than a tech trend. It's a radical departure from how the world records information. Instead of trusting middlemen, we trust math, consensus, and transparency. This chapter unpacks how it works—and why it matters.

A Public Ledger for a Trust less World

At its core, the blockchain is a ledger. Just like a notebook that tracks every dollar in and out, the blockchain records every Bitcoin transaction ever made [39]. But unlike a bank ledger locked behind closed doors, this one is open to the world [40].

Imagine a giant notebook duplicated on tens of thousands of computers across the globe [52]. Each time a new transaction occurs, the entire network agrees to add it to the next page. Once added, it's permanent. No edits. No erasing. No backdoors [40].

Each "page" of the notebook is a block. Every 10 minutes, a new block is filled with verified transactions and added to the chain [41]. Every block references the one before it, creating an unbreakable sequence—a chain of blocks. That's the blockchain [39].

It's this structure that makes the system so trustworthy. No single party can rewrite the past. Because everyone has a copy of the ledger, no one can cheat without being caught [40]. It's not about believing a trusted source—it's about verifying a trust less protocol.

Nodes: The Unsung Heroes

But who keeps all of this honest? That job falls to the nodes [39].

A node is any computer running the Bitcoin software. It doesn't need to be powerful or expensive—it just needs to be connected. Each node stores a complete copy of the blockchain and independently verifies all incoming data [40].

Nodes don't take orders from a central server. They don't rely on trust. Each one checks the math, validates the rules, and confirms whether a transaction or block is valid [39].

And here's the magic: even though these nodes operate independently, they always reach consensus. If someone tries to sneak in a fake transaction, the honest nodes reject it.

There are more than 60,000 nodes around the world today—from Buenos Aires to Brisbane, Nairobi to New York [52]. Even if thousands go offline, the network survives. That's the power of decentralisation: there is no single point of failure.

These nodes aren't just machines—they're people. Bitcoiners. Hobbyists. Teachers. Shopkeepers. Activists. Anyone with a laptop and an internet connection can download the software and join the network [40]. And once you're in, you're not just watching history—you're helping write it.

Immutable, Transparent, and Resilient

The blockchain is immutable, meaning it cannot be altered once a block is added [40]. This immutability is enforced by cryptography—every block has a unique fingerprint, or hash, which links it to the one before [53]. If someone tries to change a transaction in an old block, the entire chain breaks [39].

It's also transparent. Anyone can explore the blockchain using public tools like mempool.space [43]. You can see every transaction, every block, every movement of bitcoin—from the very first coin mined in 2009 to the one confirmed 10 minutes ago.

And it's resilient. Bitcoin's blockchain has 99.999% uptime since launch [44]. It doesn't close on weekends. It doesn't pause for holidays. It doesn't rely on a CEO, a government, or a tech support team. It doesn't even need the internet to be fully online at all times. When it comes back, it syncs, corrects, and keeps going [40].

A Living Network
Think of the blockchain like a living organism—one that grows stronger the more people interact with it [51]. Every transaction is a heartbeat. Every node is a nerve ending. Every miner is a muscle. It's a body made of code, but pulsing with human activity.

When you buy a coffee with Bitcoin, a node somewhere verifies that payment. When someone in Venezuela sends remittances to their family during hyperinflation, the blockchain records it forever [7]. When a Canadian protestor receives donations after their bank account was frozen, the network doesn't ask why [11]. It just works.

In a world where gatekeepers control access to your money, Bitcoin flips the script. With the blockchain, you are the bank. You verify your own money. You audit the supply. You see the truth [40].

Why It Matters
In traditional systems, we're forced to trust. Trust that the bank won't freeze your funds. Trust that your payment will go through. Trust that your data won't be altered.

The blockchain removes the need for trust by replacing it with verification [39]. It's not about believing—it's about checking. That's a seismic shift.

It's why Bitcoin didn't skip a beat when Greece froze ATM withdrawals in 2015 [17], or when Canada froze bank accounts during protests in 2022 [11]. The blockchain kept running. People kept transacting. No permission needed.

It's also why the network can't be easily taken down. Even if 90% of nodes disappeared overnight, the remaining 10% would carry on [52]. It's antifragile—strengthened by resistance, not weakened by it [54].

In a digital age where most systems are fragile and corruptible, the blockchain offers a new foundation—a system where rules are enforced by code, not humans [39].

Preparing for What's Next

Now that we understand what makes the blockchain so revolutionary, the next logical question is this:

If the blockchain is so powerful, why do so many cryptocurrencies fail? Why does Bitcoin endure while others fizzle out, get hacked, or become puppets for centralised insiders?

In the next chapter, we'll expose the difference between Bitcoin and the thousands of imitators. Because not all crypto is created equal—and most don't even come close.

BTC vs Altcoins

Why Bitcoin Stands Alone

Crypto is a dazzling shop—shelves stacked with shiny coins like Ethereum, Ripple, and Tether, each claiming to fix money's flaws. But here's the uncomfortable truth: most won't.
They may look like Bitcoin—but they're not.
Only one coin is built to last.
Only one is truly decentralized, with thousands of independent nodes securing its network [52].
No CEO. No central servers. No backdoors.
The rest?
They're digital fiat—tied to founders, firms, or validators who can rewrite code, pause your funds, or vanish with your money. In a crypto market ballooned to over 20,000 coins and $2 trillion in value [55], knowing the difference isn't just smart—it's survival.

So, what are these altcoins, really?
Think of them like tech startups—but without the need to register, disclose finances, or face shareholder scrutiny. Many are simply modified copies of Bitcoin's open-source code, tweaked to serve the needs of the project's creators [40].
And this is where the deeper truth kicks in.
To understand why Bitcoin stands apart, we need to grasp Proof of Work vs Proof of Stake.

🔨 Proof of Work: Earned Value

Bitcoin's protocol issues new coins roughly every 10 minutes, but not for free. They're earned. Miners around the world compete to solve cryptographic puzzles—expending real electricity, hardware, and time [42]. The winner gets rewarded with 3.125 BTC, plus the transaction fees in that block [41].

It's a system that's hard to cheat and easy to verify. This cost—real-world energy—is what anchors Bitcoin in reality. It's money you can't print at will. You must earn it.

🪙 Proof of Stake: Pre-Mined Power

Now compare that to most altcoins, which use Proof of Stake. In these systems, new coins are often pre-mined meaning the supply is created in advance, with a large portion (often over 50%) going straight to founders, insiders, and VC partners [56].

The rest? Sold to the public.

In Proof of Stake, the more coins you hold, the more power you have—effectively allowing the rich to get richer, validate their own transactions, and shape the network's rules [56]. Sound familiar?

It should. It's just central banking in crypto clothing—another system where control is concentrated at the top, and the average user is left with scraps.

Bitcoin flips that script. It rewards energy, not connections. It distributes power to anyone who runs a node or mines, regardless of location or political influence [40]. It's the only protocol built on rules, not rulers. Now that we understand the fundamental split—let's take a closer look at some of the more serious players. Because once you zoom in, the cracks in the altcoin world become hard to ignore.

Ethereum is a giant in the crypto world, powering smart contracts—digital tools that automate things like leases, loans, or crowdfunding without needing a bank. It's innovative and widely used, especially in the DeFi space [57]. But it comes with trade-offs. Just 10% of nodes control much of the network, and its founder still influences major decisions

[58]. Unlike Bitcoin, Ethereum has no fixed supply cap [59], meaning your money can be diluted over time—just like fiat. It's also been a major target for hackers, with billions lost to compromised bridges, wallets, and apps [60]. Ethereum is a powerful platform for developers—but it's not built to be a hedge. When pressure hits, it flexes. Bitcoin doesn't.

Ripple (XRP) sells itself as the solution for lightning-fast bank transfers, and its speed has attracted plenty of institutional interest. But there's a catch—it's run by a private company, Ripple Labs, which holds the majority of the coin and handpicks who gets to validate transactions [61]. That's not decentralization—it's a corporate network in disguise. When regulators stepped in and froze billions in XRP trades, holders couldn't move their funds [62]. Bitcoin, on the other hand, kept running— unstoppable, un censorable. Ripple's structure mirrors the old system: centralized, permissioned, and vulnerable to control.

Tether (USDT) is a massive stablecoin designed to mirror the U.S. dollar—$1 in, $1 out. It's great for quick payments or avoiding crypto volatility, making it handy for a $4 coffee [63]. But here's the problem: it's backed by banks and reserves that aren't always transparent. Questions have been raised about whether all the backing is truly there [64]. And if those banks stumble—like they have before—Tether could unravel fast [65]. Just like traditional fiat, it depends on trust in institutions. Bitcoin, by contrast, needs no bank and no middleman. It stands on its own, securing your value no matter what's happening behind the scenes.

Other altcoins drift in choppy waters. **Solana**, known for fast apps and low fees, has suffered multiple outages—sometimes going dark for hours—because a handful of validators hold most of the power [66]. **Cardano** mints new coins endlessly, risking the same kind of dilution that erodes fiat currencies [67]. **Binance Coin** is deeply tied to a single exchange—if that platform fails, so does the coin [68]. These projects might offer speed, flashy apps, or lower fees, but they all share one flaw: centralized control points that can break, be hacked, or shut you out. Bitcoin doesn't have those weak spots [40]. Its network is borderless, permissionless, and built to survive—no matter the storm.

Don't get us wrong altcoins can serve a purpose. Ethereum powers a vast ecosystem of digital tools, from decentralized loans to NFT marketplaces [57]. Tether is useful for everyday spending with dollar-like stability [63]. Ripple can move funds across borders faster than traditional banks [61]. But none of them are built to protect you long-term. Ethereum has been rocked by billions in hacks [60]. Tether relies on banks that may or may not hold up under pressure [64]. Ripple is steered by a private company that can be hit with lawsuits or freezes [62]. Altcoins might shine in short bursts—Solana's price booms [66], Ethereum's bull runs—but over time, they've struggled to match Bitcoin's long-term performance [69]. While others dilute, crash, or get caught in regulatory snares, Bitcoin stays scarce, secure, and unstoppable [39]. That's what makes it the king—and that isn't changing anytime soon.

Imagine you're a freelancer in a country with capital controls, landing a $200 gig. With Bitcoin, that payment is locked in—secure, immune to inflation eating it away, and untouchable by any bank [40]. No one can freeze it. No one can reverse it.

Now picture a small business owner accepting Bitcoin for a $500 order— no middleman, no 3% bank fee, just direct payment, permanently logged on a global network [39].

Choose Tether instead? You're still tied to banks that could collapse [64]. Ethereum? Its wild price swings turn your hard-earned income into a guessing game [69].

Ripple? It could stall in a courtroom while you're trying to pay rent [62]. Altcoins may wear crypto's badge, but they're just fiat dressed up— vulnerable to the same systems they claim to disrupt. When prices rise, currencies crash, or governments intervene, they don't offer protection—they buckle.

But Bitcoin? It holds.
It's your shield in the storm—backed by code, not promises. Uncensorable, un-freezable, and capped forever at 21 million coins [40]. Whether you're saving $100 for medical bills or buying a $4 coffee, Bitcoin stands firm while others fade.

This isn't theory. This is your life. Your time. Your energy.
And Bitcoin is the only money that respects it.
Fiat is collapsing under the weight of trillions in debt [20]. Altcoins flirt with the same failures—centralized teams, fragile foundations, and opaque promises [56]. Bitcoin alone stands apart—secured by thousands of machines across the globe, running with no leader, no switch to flip, no permission needed [52].

It's not flawless. It's not always fast. But it's free—free from control, inflation, and manipulation [39]. Lightning and Layer 3 apps are closing the speed gap [50], without sacrificing the core. And in a sea of 20,000 coins chasing attention [55], only one has earned the trust of millions as a fortress, not a fad.

So, if you're wondering which coin lasts—ask which one bends to no one.
Bitcoin isn't hype. It's your exit.

Is Cash Really King? BTC vs Cash

Spoiler: It's not.
Cash feels like freedom. But what if it's not the escape we think it is?

It's easy to picture it: a thick wad of cash tucked into a drawer, safe from banks, free from trackers. Some see it as the last shield against control—a simple, paper rebellion. And for a long time, it was. No app needed. No bank approval. Just bills in hand, nobody watching.
But here's the uncomfortable truth: that freedom isn't what it used to be. Not because cash changed—but because the world around it did.

We think cash is the alternative to the system—but it's the system, just folded in your pocket. It's still fiat. Still centrally controlled. Still losing value by the hour [9].
Walk into a store today and try to pay with a $50 note. In some places, the cashier smiles and takes it. In others, they point to a sign: "Card only." The shift feels subtle, almost polite. But it's not optional. It's a push. And it's everywhere.

Banks are shutting ATMs by the thousands [70]. Governments are setting targets to go "cashless" [71]. Tech giants build wallets that never touch your palm. All while quietly laying the groundwork for Central Bank Digital Currencies—CBDCs—which would make every cent trackable, programmable, and, if needed, deniable [72].
Cash isn't being replaced because it's broken. It's being replaced because it works too well.
It lets you buy things without a record. It lets you hold wealth outside the system. It lets you move money without permission.
And that makes it a problem—for them.

There was a time when cash gave people breathing room. In Greece's 2015 debt crisis, citizens lined up for hours at ATMs—limited to 60 euros a day [17]. Those with stashed cash had options. The rest waited, helpless. During COVID-19 lockdowns, some countries promoted card-only payments "for health reasons." But in many places, the shift stuck cash never quite came back [73]. In Nigeria, when citizens pushed back against a new CBDC, the government responded by limiting cash withdrawals [20]. In some cities today, a simple $10 note can be as rare as a coin from ancient Rome.

But even when you have cash, it's not what it used to be. "A $100 bill in 2000 bought what $180 does today—and try using it at a 'card only' shop [9]."
No headlines. No protest. Just steady erosion. You hold the same note, but it whispers less when you spend it.

That's the trap. People trust cash because it feels familiar. Because it feels private. Because it feels safe.
But feeling isn't fact.
We've already seen what happens when control trumps ownership.

In Cyprus, 2013, the government didn't just freeze bank accounts—they raided them. To fund a banking rescue, nearly half of large deposits were seized overnight in what became known as a "bail-in" [74]. No warning. No court. Just a flick of policy—and your money, gone.
From Lebanon's frozen accounts to Nigeria's $45-a-day cash caps, centralized systems can choke even physical money's freedom [20], [75].

These aren't flukes.
They're signals.
Whether it's a crisis, a policy shift, or a slow systemic decay, the result is the same:
If your money lives inside the system, it's never fully yours.

And it's not just about protest. Imagine needing a payment to go through and being told: "Your funds are frozen for your safety." No crime. No trial. Just a flag in a database.
This is where the illusion of cash breaks down. It's not a shield. It's a bubble. And it's getting smaller.

Now, bring in Bitcoin. Not as hype. Not as speculation. But as a real answer to the question:

If cash stops working, what's left?

Bitcoin doesn't replace cash by acting like cash. It replaces cash by doing what cash was supposed to do—and then going further.

It lets you send $4 for coffee—instantly, with no middleman, no surveillance. Just a scan, and done [50].

It lets you store $100 that can't be printed away, can't be devalued by policy, can't be shut off because of your job, your views, or your politics [40].

It lets you send $200 to someone across the world, no questions asked, no border agents, no 3-day wire fees.

Bitcoin doesn't ask for permission. It doesn't need a name. It doesn't care if the bank is closed.

It's cash with a backbone.

Where cash is losing ground, Bitcoin is gaining strength.

It can't be demonetized. It doesn't care what country you're in. And it doesn't shrink when politicians panic.

To be clear, it's not perfect. Bitcoin's price can swing. It can take time to learn.

But the freedom it gives isn't a theory—it's tested, and it's real.

Attributes of your Assets

	Cash	Gold	House	Bitcoin
SCARCE		✓	✓	✓
UNINFLATABLE				✓
PORTABLE	✓			✓
DURABLE	✓	✓	✓	✓
INTERNATIONAL		✓		✓
FUNGIBLE	✓	✓		✓
DIVISIBLE	✓	✓		✓
VERIFIED SUPPLY			✓	✓
DECENTRALISED				✓
CONFISCATABLE	✓	✓	✓	✗

In Argentina, where inflation shattered people's savings, Bitcoin became a lifeline [77]. In Nigeria, where cash withdrawals were throttled, Bitcoin kept moving [20]. In Ukraine, as war scattered lives, Bitcoin brought in aid faster than banks ever could [78].

While governments test $1 billion in CBDC programs [79], people are scanning $4 coffees with Bitcoin's Lightning Network [76], skipping the entire system.

While central banks rehearse control, 150 million people now use Bitcoin to escape it [80].

This is the shift unfolding now.
Cash got us far. It gave us years of freedom, privacy, and ease.
But it's leaving the stage.
The new fight isn't cash vs cards—it's permission vs permissionless.
Fiat—whether paper or plastic—is built on rules you don't control.
Bitcoin flips that. It gives you a vault in your pocket, a network that
doesn't sleep, and a payment system that doesn't discriminate.

You don't need to burn your bills or toss your coins. But understand
what they are: relics of a system slipping deeper into surveillance.
As more stores go cashless and more governments embrace CBDCs,
your $50 note might feel like comfort—but it's a comfort with an
expiration date.

Bitcoin doesn't just preserve what cash used to offer—it pushes it
further.
In a world turning cashless, it's the last true exit from financial
surveillance.
Not because it looks like money, but because it behaves like freedom.
And soon, it might be the only thing that can.

"The state is a criminal organisation that lives off a coercive source of income called taxes. In Reality its a large scale criminal organisation. Worse than the common thief. Do the Math : How many times does a common thief rob you in 1 year. The State steals from you every day, it steals from you every day all the time."

JAVIER MILEI

Digital Traps: Future of Currency Is Already Here

It starts with a simple tap—a $4 coffee. You wave your phone, expecting the familiar beep. But the screen flashes red: "Transaction declined." Your account has funds. No issue on your end. Then the message appears: "Carbon limit exceeded spending paused until next month." Your stomach drops. You laugh, hoping it's a glitch. But deep down, you know it's not. This is your money, but someone else decides when it works.

This isn't a distant threat—it's happening now. In China, a full-scale social credit system, powered by digital payments, tracks and scores every purchase, every post, every step you take [79]. Millions are locked out of trains, planes, or loans—not for crimes, but for behaviours the government deems unacceptable, like criticizing a policy or buying too much alcohol. One wrong move online, and your digital wallet shuts off. Your life, paused. This is the reality of programmable money, and it's already here.

China's model is spreading—not with tanks, but with apps promising convenience. In 2018, the World Economic Forum outlined a future where every click, purchase, or social connection feeds a "financial access score" [81]. Your money's usability hinges on your behaviour—say the wrong thing, and your account could freeze. Over 80 governments are quietly adopting this blueprint, disguising control behind terms like "financial inclusion" or "innovative payments" [72]. It's not coming—it's already rolling out.

They're not calling it a social credit system, but at its core, it mirrors exactly what's already happening in China [79]. And the key component—the mechanism that makes it all possible—is the Central Bank Digital Currency, or CBDC. CBDCs are not just digital versions of the dollars or euros you already use. They're programmable [72]. That means your government can dictate when, where, or how your money is used. Want to buy a second burger this week? Maybe your health limit won't allow it. Spend too much on fuel? That could trigger a carbon penalty. Post a tweet that doesn't align with state messaging? Don't be surprised if your wallet stops working.

These aren't conspiracies. They're features. Built in.

This new financial layer is spreading fast, echoing China's playbook. Nigeria's eNaira tracks every transaction, limiting spending freedom and paving the way for programmable restrictions [20].

The EU's "Digital Euro" merges identity and spending, tracking every transaction [78]. Australia is dismantling ATMs, nudging people toward digital control [70]. In India, 86% of cash was demonetized overnight in 2016, pushing digital payments and setting the stage for CBDC control [82].

In every case, CBDC pilots, backed by the Bank for International Settlements, are paving the way for programmable money that answers to the state [78].

The trap is already set. And it's dressed in the language of progress.

They'll say it's more efficient. They'll say it reduces fraud. They'll promise faster tax refunds and instant welfare payments. But all of that comes at a cost: your autonomy.

Once your money becomes conditional, it's no longer yours. This is where Bitcoin enters—not as an alternative, but as a lifeline.

Bitcoin doesn't care who you are, what you believe, or how you spend [40]. It doesn't require approval. It doesn't freeze, expire, or ask for ID. Whether it's $4 for coffee, $100 in savings, or $200 sent to another country, Bitcoin enables you to move value freely. With the Lightning Network, payments are instant, cheap, and private [76]. With self-custody wallets like BlueWallet or Phoenix, you hold your money directly—no bank necessary [83].

Bitcoin is not built for compliance. It's built for freedom.

It doesn't replace fiat by mimicking its systems. It replaces fiat by rejecting its controls. Let's compare the two.

CBDCs are owned, issued, and managed by central authorities. They can be frozen, programmed, or tracked. Their existence depends on your government's trust in you. They are designed for surveillance.

Bitcoin is decentralized, borderless, and permissionless. It can't be stopped, altered, or manipulated. Your Bitcoin belongs to you, and you alone. No one else has access—not a government, not a company, not a central bank.

The contrast is staggering.

Feature	CBDC	Bitcoin
Controlled by	Central Bank / Government (Bank for International Settlements, 2023)[98]	No one (Nakamoto, 2008)[67]
Requires ID	Yes (Bank for International Settlements, 2023)[98]	No (Nakamoto, 2008)[67]
Privacy	None (Bank for International Settlements, 2023)[98]	Yes (Nakamoto, 2008)[67]
Can expire	Yes (Bank for International Settlements, 2023)[98]	No (Nakamoto, 2008)[67]
Can be frozen	Yes (Bank for International Settlements, 2023)[98]	No (Nakamoto, 2008)[67]
Usage rules	Defined by state (Bank for International Settlements, 2023)[98]	None (Nakamoto, 2008)[67]
Borderless?	No (Bank for International Settlements, 2023)[98]	Yes (Nakamoto, 2008)[67]
Fees?	Variable, may include taxes (Bank for International Settlements, 2023)[98]	Low or none (Nakamoto, 2008)[67]

The WEF wants programmable money [81]. Bitcoin is unprogrammable value. CBDCs are designed to serve the system. Bitcoin is designed to serve the individual.

Most people won't see it coming. CBDCs will arrive wrapped in promises—free credits, cashback, "greener" payments, seamless ID integration. But one day, you'll buy the wrong book, support the wrong cause, or post the wrong opinion—and your money will stop working. In China, this is already daily life [79]. Elsewhere, it's closer than you think. Act now, or it'll be too late.

Using Bitcoin—even in small ways—teaches you to exit the system quietly. Not in protest, but in power. Every Lightning transaction is a statement: I control my wealth. Every $50 saved outside a bank is a vote against the surveillance economy. Every international payment made without permission is a crack in the wall they're building.

Bitcoin doesn't need to be perfect. It just needs to be yours.

You can't fix fiat. You can't trust CBDCs.

But you can opt out.

The trap is already here. But so is the key. Hold it tight. Use it well. Build something unbreakable.

Controlling Your Own Wealth

By now, you've seen the system for what it really is—how money is being reshaped into a tool of control.

You've watched the transition from physical notes to digital scores, from savings accounts to state-managed wallets. And you've seen that the future isn't something coming next decade. It's already here. The next question is: What do you do about it?

Owning Bitcoin isn't just about investing or speculating. It's about control. It's about owning your wealth in a way that no bank, no government, no central authority can alter, freeze, or manipulate. It's about knowing that your money is truly yours—accessible, spendable, and secure, with no one standing between you and your freedom.

For most of your life, "wealth" has meant whatever the bank says is in your account. But that balance is a number someone else controls. It can be limited, denied, drained by fees, or frozen entirely—sometimes just because your government doesn't like what you've said or done. In a world moving toward programmable money and surveillance spending, the idea of owning your wealth has become a myth. Bitcoin makes real again.

Let's start small.

You download a simple app—BlueWallet, Phoenix, or Muun [83][84].
You scan a QR code and buy $10 worth of Bitcoin. Within seconds, that value is yours. Not in a bank. Not on a permissioned ledger. Not tied to your name or tax file number. Just sitting in your digital wallet, ready to spend, send, or save as you choose. It's as easy as topping up a prepaid phone.

Now imagine using $4 of that balance to buy a coffee from a local shop that accepts Bitcoin via the Lightning Network [76]. You tap, scan, confirm—done. No approval process. No bank server. No risk of being flagged for buying the "wrong" product or going over some limit you didn't even know existed. It just works.

And that's what real ownership feels like.
No one can see the transaction unless you want them to. No one can stop it. It wasn't tracked, scored, or logged into a profile for advertisers or institutions. That $4 wasn't just spent—it was wielded. Controlled. Liberated.

Let's scale it up.
Say you have $100 set aside for savings. In a fiat bank account, that $100 is bleeding value everyday thanks to inflation [9]. You're not being rewarded for saving. You're being punished for it. Meanwhile, that $100 can be restricted, taxed, or even seized if something in your life trips a system alarm. Whether it's a fine you forgot about, a protest you joined, or a donation flagged as suspicious, your funds can be frozen without warning.

Now put that same $100 into Bitcoin.
You hold the private keys. You decide when and how to access it. No institution can touch it. It's not just savings—it's sovereignty. And with proper security practices (like using a hardware wallet or multisig setup), that $100 can be locked down tighter than any bank vault [85].

This is wealth that lives with you. Not "accessible" via terms and conditions but owned.

Then there's the $200 scenario—the one that breaks borders. Imagine you're a freelancer being paid for work across continents. A traditional bank wire costs up to $30 in fees and takes 2–3 days, assuming nothing gets flagged along the way [79]. With Bitcoin, you send that $200 directly to your client, or receive it from them, in minutes, for mere cents. No banks. No friction. No exposure to government exchange controls or institutional delays.

Now flip the script.
Imagine you're helping family overseas—people living under unstable governments, in collapsing economies, or in countries where access to the global financial system is tightly restricted. Bitcoin lets you bypass all of it. You send support instantly, securely, and privately. No borders. No begging a remittance service to accept your ID. No 10% cut from a wire agency.

You just help them.
That's the kind of control fiat can never offer.

The Road Ahead

The storm's here—and there's no use pretending otherwise.

For decades, governments and central banks kicked the can down the road. Now we're at the end of it.
Global debt stands at over $300 trillion—a number so large it's almost meaningless [23]. Every nation is bleeding red ink. Inflation eats into every paycheck [9]. Pensions wobble. Trust erodes. The average citizen, once promised stability, is now left managing survival.

This is the mess fiat built.
But amid the noise, something else grows—quiet, steady, unstoppable.
Bitcoin.

With roughly 150 million users worldwide and counting [80], Bitcoin isn't just surviving—it's thriving. It doesn't rely on a boardroom. It doesn't bend to political whim. It just keeps ticking, every ten minutes, a block at a time.

That reliability matters.
In a world full of deceit, something true is revolutionary.

We're no longer talking about fringe developers or libertarian theorists. We're talking about everyday people—families in Argentina fleeing hyperinflation [77], Ukrainians crossing borders with their wealth in a wallet only they can access [79], and Gen Z Australians stacking sats between Uber shifts [80].

The sovereign individual is being born in real time.
And this movement isn't about greed. It's about exit.
Not escape from responsibility but exit from abuse. From unsound money. From centralized control. From surveillance sold as safety.

It's about regaining dignity in how we earn, save, and build.
Because we know this system isn't going to fix itself. They've proven

that.

Every financial crash.

Every "too big to fail."

Every quiet bailout [65].

Every headline about record profits while households drown.

Bitcoin doesn't claim to solve all of that—but it gives people a way to opt out.

A new path. A parallel system. Not imposed but chosen.

No leader. No permission.

Just code, consensus, and conviction.

And yes, it's still early. Bitcoin's reach may be growing, but the world is still asleep lulled by comfort, seduced by credit, distracted by noise.

But that's changing.

With every currency devaluation, with every authoritarian overreach, more people look for a way out. And they find it. Not through protest. Not through politics. Through protocol.

The revolution will not be televised—it will be verified.

Block by block. Wallet by wallet. Person by person.

The question is no longer *if* this system fails. It's *when*—and who's ready.

Bitcoin doesn't promise utopia. But it offers a foundation.

And foundations are how you rebuild after the storm.

No heroes. No shortcuts.

Just you. Just us.

And one tool—truth, in digital form.

Ready?

The Power is Yours

You've made it. You've unravelled the truth about money—a system that's been quietly working against you, your family, your future. But this isn't about what you've lost. It's about what you've gained: the knowledge to take back control.

Bitcoin isn't just a currency; it's your key to a world where you decide what your money does, where it goes, and who gets to touch it [39]. You're not just a reader anymore—you're a builder, ready to shape a future that answers to you.

Bitcoin isn't just a tool—it's your tool. It's the key to a door you didn't even know existed until now. Armed with the knowledge from this book, you're no longer a bystander in a system designed to limit you. You're a builder of your own future, equipped with a currency that answers to no one but you [39].

This is your moment.

Bitcoin is more than code or cryptography—it's a declaration of independence in a world that demands dependence. Its design is your shield: borderless, permissionless, and deflationary by nature [40]. Every Satoshi you hold is a stake in a new reality, one where you control your wealth, your choices, and your time. Every transaction you make is a vote for a system built on transparency, not manipulation; on freedom, not control.

The world may still misunderstand Bitcoin. They'll call it volatile, speculative, or risky. But you know better. You see what they don't: the early internet was mocked, too, until it reshaped existence. Bitcoin is that same kind of revolution, growing stronger every day, every block, every node. And you're not just along for the ride—you're driving it.

This isn't about chasing quick riches. It's about claiming long-term sovereignty. It's about dignity. It's about owning your time in a world that's always trying to take it.

You hold the private key to something bigger than money. You hold the power to say no to a system that was never built for you [19]. Bitcoin is your life raft, your foundation, your chance to stand firm as the old-world creaks under its own weight.

So, take it. Use it. Build with it. Not because it's trendy, but because it's the most honest tool we have. The question isn't "Why Bitcoin?" anymore—it's "What will you do with it?"

The Power Is Yours—Make It Count

Don't just watch history—write it.
Don't wait for permission—choose your freedom.
Don't just hope for change—help build it.

The world is changing. The power is yours.

Final Note

You don't need to predict the future to prepare for it.
You've seen what's broken, and you've seen what's possible.
The next step isn't waiting — it's learning, stacking, and teaching others.
Because every person who understands Bitcoin helps restore honesty to money itself.

Start small. Tell one person. Hold one sat. That's how revolutions begin.

APPENDIX A: Bitcoin Is Power — If You're Ready.

You've seen how the system is rigged—how money is printed, inflated, and controlled. You've discovered how Bitcoin offers a way out: fixed, transparent, decentralized. Not just a new kind of money, but a new kind of trust.

But before you rush off to buy your first Bitcoin or stack your first sats, let's get real:

Bitcoin doesn't save you. You save yourself.

Bitcoin hands you the tools. But tools only work if you pick them up and use them responsibly.

This isn't hype. This is your wake-up call.

Because with Bitcoin, there's no cavalry coming if you mess up.
No customer service hotline.
No "forgot password" email reset.
No banker to fix a mistake.

That's the trade-off.
In a world where banks and governments play God with your money, Bitcoin puts the power back in your hands.
But with power comes responsibility.

The Basics: Getting Started the Right Way

This isn't financial advice.
It's sovereignty advice.
You're not just buying Bitcoin. You're stepping into personal responsibility for your money—maybe for the first time in your life.

Let's walk through the essentials:

✅ Step 1: Buy a Small Amount

You don't need to buy a whole Bitcoin. You can start with $10, $50, or whatever feels manageable.

How to begin:

1. **Choose a reputable exchange in your country:**

   - AU Australia: BTC Markets, Swyftx, HardBlock

   - US USA: Swan Bitcoin, River, Strike, Cash App

   - 🌏 Global: Kraken, Binance (but always withdraw to your own wallet)

2. **Create an account.** (Yes, you'll need to provide ID—thanks to "Know Your Customer" laws.)

3. **Link your bank account or debit card.**

4. **Buy Bitcoin (BTC)—even $10 is enough to begin.**

💬 *This is your first exposure. Treat it like training wheels.*

✅ Step 2: Withdraw Immediately

Get your BTC **off the exchange**.

Why?

- If the exchange collapses, your Bitcoin is gone.

- If a government demands they freeze withdrawals, they will.

- If a hacker gets in, you're left holding the bag.

Not your keys, not your coins.

How to withdraw:

1. **Download a self-custody wallet (non-custodial = you control the keys):**

   o Beginner: Muun, Phoenix, BlueWallet [83][84]

   o Advanced: Sparrow, Electrum

2. **Set up your wallet.**

   o Write down your 12- or 24-word seed phrase (this is your backup—never share it).

   o Never store it on your phone or computer. Write it on paper and keep it safe.

3. **Copy your receiving address from your wallet and paste it into the exchange's withdrawal page.**

4. **Withdraw your BTC.** It may take 10–30 minutes to confirm.

🎯 *Congratulations. You now control your first sovereign Bitcoin.*

✅ **Step 3: Learn to Protect It**

Owning Bitcoin means nothing if you lose it or mismanage it.
Your seed phrase = your vault key.

- Lose it? Your BTC is gone forever.

- Someone finds it. They can steal your BTC.

Tips:

- Store your seed phrase offline (on paper or metal, not a photo).

- Make at least two copies, kept in separate secure locations (safe, lockbox, etc).

- Do small test transactions—send a few dollars of BTC to another wallet to build your confidence [85].

✅ Step 4: Consider a Hardware Wallet

Once your holdings grow past a few hundred dollars, **upgrade your security**.

- Devices like Coldcard, Trezor, or Blockstream Jade. Keep your private keys offline [85].

- They protect you from hacks, malware, phishing attempts, and phone theft.

Start with a mobile wallet to learn. Move to a hardware wallet when you're confident.

✅ Step 5: Keep Learning—Forever

Bitcoin is not "set and forget."
The protocol is stable—but tools and threats evolve.
Stay sharp:

- **Read books:** *The Bitcoin Standard, Layered Money, The Price of Tomorrow.*

- **Listen to podcasts:** Stephan Livera, BTC Sessions, Natalie Brunell.

- **Follow voices who teach sovereignty, not hype or trading.**

♡ Bitcoin doesn't require perfection, but it demands respect.

🗣 The Mental Shift: No One's Coming to Save You

With fiat, the government insures your bank—until it doesn't.
With Bitcoin, you are the bank.

- **You are the security.**

- **You are the custodian.**

- **You are the last line of defence.**

That means:

- You don't "invest" in Bitcoin the same way you buy stocks.

- You don't chase price spikes.

- You don't forget your backups.

You take ownership. Slowly. Deliberately. Intentionally.

⚠️ What Bitcoin Can't Do

- Bitcoin won't fix poor spending habits.

- It won't stop you from gambling on altcoins.

- It won't save your family if you don't first save yourself from emotional decisions.

Bitcoin is a mirror.
It reflects your patience, your self-control, your discipline.

If you want a quick dopamine hit—go gamble.
If you want to build lasting wealth—build discipline.

🔚 Final Word: Take It Seriously, or Leave It Alone

Bitcoin gives you freedom—but only if you're ready to carry the weight of that freedom.

And here's the hard truth:
Some people aren't ready. That's okay. But understand what's at stake.

Fiat won't protect you.
CBDCs won't empower you.
Time won't wait.

You don't need to be perfect.
But you do need to be intentional.

This book isn't asking you to trust us.
It's asking you to trust yourself.

Because now, you can see the game being played around you.
And for the first time—you have the tools to step off the board.

The question now is simple:
Will you use them?

Crypto & Bitcoin Glossary

Altcoin: Any cryptocurrency that is not Bitcoin. Examples: Ethereum, Solana, Cardano.

Bitcoin: The first and most well-known decentralized digital currency, created by Satoshi Nakamoto in 2009.

Blockchain: A public digital ledger that records all Bitcoin transactions in a way that can't be changed or tampered with.

CBDC (Central Bank Digital Currency): A digital version of a country's currency issued and controlled by the central bank—programmable and often trackable.

Cold Wallet / Hardware Wallet: A physical device (like a USB stick) that stores your Bitcoin offline for security.

Custodial Wallet: A wallet where a third party (like an exchange) holds your Bitcoin for you (they hold the keys, not you).

dApp (Decentralized Application): An app that runs on a blockchain rather than a single server, meaning no one entity controls it.

Decentralized: Not controlled by any single person, company, or government—power is spread across many people or computers.

DeFi (Decentralized Finance): Financial services (like lending, trading, borrowing) run by code on a blockchain, not a bank.

Fiat Money: Government-issued currency not backed by anything physical (like gold). Examples: US Dollar, Euro, Australian Dollar.

FOMO (Fear of Missing Out): The anxious feeling that you'll miss out on potential profits if you don't invest now.

FUD (Fear, Uncertainty, Doubt): Negative rumours or news meant to scare people into selling or avoiding crypto.

Halving: The event (about every 4 years) when the amount of new Bitcoin created and earned by miners is cut in half. Makes Bitcoin scarcer over time.

HODL: A typo for "hold" that became slang for holding on to Bitcoin through ups and downs, not selling under pressure.

KYC (Know Your Customer): Regulations that require exchanges and banks to check your ID before letting you buy/sell crypto.

Layer 2: Technology built on top of Bitcoin to make it faster or cheaper to use (like the Lightning Network).

Ledger: A record of all transactions (think of it as the ultimate accounting book).

Lightning Network: A way to send Bitcoin instantly and with very low fees by settling many small payments off-chain and then recording the net result on the blockchain.

Mining: The process of securing Bitcoin's network and creating new coins by solving complex computer puzzles.

Multisig (Multi-signature): A security system where more than one person or device must approve a transaction before it goes through.

Node: A computer that keeps a copy of the Bitcoin blockchain and helps verify transactions.

Non-custodial Wallet / Self-Custody: A wallet where *you* control the keys (passwords) to your Bitcoin, not any company or exchange.

Private Key / Seed Phrase: Your secret password (usually 12 or 24 words) that lets you access and move your Bitcoin. If you lose this, you lose your coins.

Proof of Work: The system Bitcoin uses, where miners do real-world work (using electricity) to validate transactions.

Proof of Stake: A different system (used by many altcoins) where the more coins you hold, the more you can help run the network.

Public Key / Address: Like your bank account number for receiving Bitcoin—safe to share, but not to spend from.

Sats / Satoshi's: The smallest unit of Bitcoin. 1 Bitcoin = 100,000,000 sats. "Sats" is like "cents" for dollars.

Seed Phrase: See "Private Key." The master password for your wallet.

Smart Contract: Code that runs on a blockchain and does things automatically (like release payment when conditions are met).

Stablecoin: A cryptocurrency that tries to keep its value stable, usually by being tied to the dollar or another asset.

Wallet: Software or hardware that stores your Bitcoin addresses and private keys so you can send and receive coins.

MASTER REFERENCE INDEX –

CHAPTER 1 MASTER REFERENCE INDEX

1. Grant, M. (1976). *The Roman Economy: Studies in Ancient Economic and Administrative History*. Penguin Books.

2. Ebrey, P. B. (2010). *The Cambridge Illustrated History of China* (2nd ed.). Cambridge University Press.

3. Hamilton, E. J. (1934). *American Treasure and the Price Revolution in Spain, 1501–1650*. Harvard University Press.

4. Kindleberger, C. P. (2005). *Manias, Panics, and Crashes: A History of Financial Crises* (5th ed.). Wiley.

5. Fergusson, A. (2010). *When Money Dies: The Nightmare of Deficit Spending, Devaluation, and Hyperinflation in Weimar Germany*. PublicAffairs.

6. Hanke, S. H., & Kwok, A. F. (2009). On the Measurement of Zimbabwe's Hyperinflation. *Cato Journal*, 29(2), 353–364.

7. International Monetary Fund. (2019). Venezuela: Staff Report for the 2019 Article IV Consultation. IMF Country Report No. 19/13.

8. Nixon, R. M. (1971, August 15). Address to the nation outlining a new economic policy: "The challenge of peace." *The American Presidency Project*.

9. U.S. Bureau of Labor Statistics. (2023). Consumer Price Index inflation calculator. https://www.bls.gov/data/inflation_calculator.htm

CHAPTER 2: Master Reference Index (continued)

10. U.S. Department of the Treasury. (2020). Economic Impact Payment Information Center. https://www.irs.gov/coronavirus/economic-impact-payment-information-center

11. U.S. Federal Reserve. (2022). Federal Reserve Statistical Release—H.6 Money Stock Measures. https://www.federalreserve.gov/releases/h6/current/

12. Reserve Bank of Australia. (2023). Statement on Monetary Policy—May 2023. https://www.rba.gov.au/publications/smp/

13. Bank of England. (2023). Sterling exchange rates and UK economic data 2023. https://www.bankofengland.co.uk/statistics

14. Ammous, S. (2018). The Bitcoin Standard: The Decentralized Alternative to Central Banking. Wiley.

15. Zillow. (2023). Median Home Value in the United States. https://www.zillow.com/research/data/

(References [7], [9] reused from earlier chapters, new numbers continue sequentially for newly introduced sources.)

Chapter 3: Master Reference Index (continued)

16. International Monetary Fund. (2002). Argentina: Staff report for the 2001 Article IV consultation (pp. 12–15). IMF Country Report No. 02/77. https://www.imf.org/en/Publications/CR/Issues/2002/04/02/Argentina-2001-Article-IV-Consultation-16547

17. European Central Bank. (2015). Greek debt crisis: Financial stability review 2015. https://www.ecb.europa.eu/pub/pdf/fsr/financialstabilityreview201511.en.pdf

18. Turkish Statistical Institute. (2022). Consumer Price Index: Annual report 2022. https://data.tuik.gov.tr/Bulten/Index?p=Consumer-Price-Index-2022-45866

(References [7] and [11] reused from earlier chapters for Venezuela and Canada; all numbers continue in order and are unique.)

Chapter 4: Master Reference Index (continued)

19. International Monetary Fund. (2023). Global Financial Stability Report: 2023. https://www.imf.org/en/Publications/GFSR

20. Organisation for Economic Co-operation and Development. (2023). Economic Outlook 2023. https://www.oecd.org/economic-outlook

21. Australian Bureau of Statistics. (2023). Consumer Price Index: June 2023. https://www.abs.gov.au/statistics/economy/price-indexes-and-inflation/consumer-price-index-australia/jun-2023

22. U.S. Department of Agriculture. (2023). Food price outlook: 2023–2024 projections. https://www.ers.usda.gov/data-products/food-price-outlook/

23. U.S. Treasury. (2020). Economic Impact Payment Information Center. https://www.irs.gov/coronavirus/economic-impact-payment-information-center

24. U.S. Census Bureau. (2022). Lumber Price Data. https://www.census.gov/construction/nrs/pdf/price.pdf

25. U.S. Bureau of Labor Statistics. (2023). Wage and Price Data 2020–2023. https://www.bls.gov/data/

26. National Coffee Association. (2023). Coffee market trends and prices. https://www.ncausa.org/Research-Trends

27. Zillow. (2023). Median Rent Index. https://www.zillow.com/research/data/

28. Sporting Goods Manufacturers Association. (2023). Price Trends: Sporting Goods. https://sgma.com/research/

29. World Bank. (2023). Poverty and Equity Database. https://povertydata.worldbank.org/

30. Federal Reserve. (2023). Interest Rate Decisions. https://www.federalreserve.gov/monetarypolicy.htm

31. Freddie Mac. (2023). 30-Year Fixed Rate Mortgage Data. https://www.freddiemac.com/pmms/

32. U.S. Small Business Administration. (2023). Small Business Lending Statistics. https://www.sba.gov/about-sba/open-government/digital-sba/open-data/small-business-lending-statistics

33. Bank of Japan. (2023). Historical Statistics. https://www.boj.or.jp/en/statistics/

(References [5], [7], [9], [10], [11], [13], [16], [21], [22], etc., are reused as appropriate; all numbers unique and continuous throughout the manuscript.)

Chapter 5: Master Reference Index (continued)

34. Eurostat. (2022). Energy Price Statistics. https://ec.europa.eu/eurostat/statistics-explained/index.php?title=Energy_price_statistics

35. International Monetary Fund. (2022). Argentina: Staff Report for the 2022 Article IV Consultation. https://www.imf.org/en/Publications/CR/Issues/2022/12/16/Argentina-2022-Article-IV-Consultation-524778

36. Central Bank of Sri Lanka. (2023). Annual Report 2022. https://www.cbsl.gov.lk/en/publications/economic-and-financial-reports/annual-reports

37. Congressional Budget Office. (2023). The Budget and Economic Outlook: 2023 to 2033. https://www.cbo.gov/publication/58848

38. Gallup. (2023). Americans' Confidence in Major U.S. Institutions. https://news.gallup.com/poll/1597/confidence-institutions.aspx

(References [19], [20], [29], [30] are reused from earlier chapters; all numbers unique and continuous.)

Chapter 6: Master Reference Index (continued)

39. Nakamoto, S. (2008). Bitcoin: A Peer-to-Peer Electronic Cash System (Bitcoin white paper). https://bitcoin.org/bitcoin.pdf

40. Antonopoulos, A. M. (2017). Mastering Bitcoin: Unlocking Digital Cryptocurrencies (2nd ed.). O'Reilly Media.

41. Bitcoin.org. (2024). How does Bitcoin work? https://bitcoin.org/en/how-it-works

42. De Vries, A. (2018). Bitcoin's Growing Energy Problem. Joule, 2(5), 801–805.

43. Mempool.Space (2024). Bitcoin Blockchain Explorer. https://mempool.space

44. Bitnodes.io (2024). Bitcoin Network Uptime Statistics. https://bitnodes.io

45. CoinDesk. (2023). Bitcoiners Turn Greenpeace's 'Skull of Satoshi' Into a Mascot. https://www.coindesk.com/policy/2023/03/24/bitcoiners-turn-greenpeaces-skull-of-satoshi-into-a-mascot/

46. Krause, M. J., & Tolaymat, T. (2018). Quantification of energy and carbon costs for mining cryptocurrencies. Nature Sustainability, 1(11), 711–718.

47. Narayanan, A., Bonneau, J., Felten, E., Miller, A., & Goldfeder, S. (2016). Bitcoin and Cryptocurrency Technologies. Princeton University Press.

48. Buterin, V. (2015). On Public and Private Blockchains. Ethereum Foundation Blog. https://blog.ethereum.org/2015/08/07/on-public-and-private-blockchains/

49. Zamyatin, A., Al-Bassam, M., et al. (2021). SoK: Communication Across Distributed Ledgers. arXiv preprint arXiv:2102.09549.

50. Lightning Labs. (2024). Lightning Network Overview. https://lightning.network/

51. Tapscott, D., & Tapscott, A. (2016). Blockchain Revolution: How the Technology Behind Bitcoin and Other Cryptocurrencies is Changing the World. Portfolio.

52. Luke Dashjr. (2024). Global Bitcoin Node Count. https://luke.dashjr.org/programs/bitcoin/files/charts/historical.html

(References [19], [20], [29], [38], etc. are reused from earlier chapters.)

Chapter 7: Master Reference Index (continued)

53. Narayanan, A., Bonneau, J., Felten, E., Miller, A., & Goldfeder, S. (2016). *Bitcoin and Cryptocurrency Technologies*. Princeton University Press.

54. Taleb, N. N. (2012). *Antifragile: Things That Gain from Disorder*. Random House.

(References [7], [11], [17], [39], [40], [41], [43], [44], [51], [52] are reused from earlier chapters.)

Chapter 8: Master Reference Index (continued)

55. CoinMarketCap. (2025). Cryptocurrency Market Capitalizations. https://coinmarketcap.com

56. Gensler, G. (2021). Remarks Before the Aspen Security Forum: Cryptocurrencies and Decentralized Finance. U.S. Securities and Exchange Commission. https://www.sec.gov/news/speech/gensler-aspen-security-forum-2021

57. Ethereum Foundation. (2024). What is Ethereum? https://ethereum.org/en/what-is-ethereum/

58. Etherscan. (2024). Ethereum Node Distribution. https://etherscan.io/nodetracker

59. Ethereum Foundation. (2024). Ethereum Monetary Policy. https://ethereum.org/en/developers/docs/monetary-policy/

60. Chainalysis. (2024). Crypto Crime Report. https://www.chainalysis.com/blog/crypto-crime-2024/

61. Ripple Labs. (2024). RippleNet Overview. https://ripple.com/ripplenet/

62. U.S. Securities and Exchange Commission. (2023). SEC v. Ripple Labs, Inc. https://www.sec.gov/litigation/litreleases/2023/lr25682.htm

63. Tether. (2024). Transparency. https://tether.to/en/transparency/

64. CoinDesk. (2024). Tether Reserves Audit Raises Questions. https://www.coindesk.com/business/2024/03/20/tether-audit-questions/

65. Federal Reserve. (2008). The Financial Crisis Inquiry Report. https://www.federalreserve.gov/publications/other-reports/files/financial-crisis-inquiry-report.pdf

66. Solana Foundation. (2023). Network Performance and Incidents. https://status.solana.com

67. Cardano Foundation. (2024). ADA Supply. https://cardano.org/supply/

68. Binance. (2024). About Binance Coin (BNB). https://www.binance.com/en/bnb

69. CoinGecko. (2025). Cryptocurrency Returns and Volatility. https://coingecko.com/en/returns

(References [20], [39], [40], [41], [42], [50], [52], etc. reused from earlier chapters.)

Chapter 9: Master Reference Index (continued)

70. Australian Broadcasting Corporation. (2023). Why are so many ATMs disappearing from Australian streets? https://www.abc.net.au/news/2023-07-24/atms-disappearing-cashless-australia/102636622

71. Reserve Bank of Australia. (2024). Payments System Board Annual Report. https://www.rba.gov.au/publications/annual-reports/psb/2024/

72. Bank for International Settlements. (2023). CBDCs: Opportunities, risks and policy considerations. https://www.bis.org/publ/arpdf/ar2023e3.htm

73. The Guardian. (2021). COVID-19 accelerates the decline of cash. https://www.theguardian.com/world/2021/jan/05/covid-pandemic-accelerates-the-decline-of-cash

74. European Central Bank. (2013). The Cyprus Bail-in: A Unique Solution. https://www.ecb.europa.eu/pub/pdf/other/eb201304en.pdf

75. World Bank. (2021). Lebanon: Financial Crisis and Impacts. https://www.worldbank.org/en/news/feature/2021/11/29/lebanon-financial-crisis-facts

76. Lightning Labs. (2024). Lightning Network Growth and Usage. https://lightning.network/

77. Central Bank of Argentina. (2023). Inflation and Bitcoin Adoption Report. https://www.bcra.gov.ar/Pdfs/PublicacionesEstadisticas/BitcoinArgentina2023.pdf

78. UNICEF. (2022). Crypto Donations Bring Fast Aid to Ukraine. https://www.unicef.org/ukraine/en/stories/crypto-donations-aid-ukraine

79. Bank for International Settlements. (2023). CBDC Tracker. https://www.bis.org/cbdc/

80. Chainalysis. (2023). Global Crypto Adoption Index 2023. https://blog.chainalysis.com/reports/2023-global-crypto-adoption-index/

(References [9], [17], [20], [40], [50], etc., are reused from earlier chapters.)

Chapter 10: Master Reference Index (continued)

81. World Economic Forum. (2018). The Future of Financial Infrastructure: An Ambitious Look at How Blockchain Can Reshape Financial Services. https://www.weforum.org/agenda/2018/06/the-future-of-financial-infrastructure/

82. Reserve Bank of India. (2016). Withdrawal of Legal Tender Status for ₹500 and ₹1000 Notes: RBI Circular. https://www.rbi.org.in/Scripts/BS_PressReleaseDisplay.aspx?prid=38520

83. Blue Wallet & Phoenix. (2023). Self-Custody Lightning Wallets. https://bluewallet.io | https://phoenix.acinq.co

References reused from Chapters 1–9:
[20], [40], [70], [72], [76], [78], [79]

Chapter 11: Master Reference Index (continued)

New references for Chapter 11:
84. Muun. (2023). Bitcoin and Lightning Wallet. https://www.muun.com
85. Kaspersky. (2023). How to Store Cryptocurrency Safely: Hardware Wallets and Multisig Explained. https://www.kaspersky.com/blog/crypto-storage-security/47349/

References [9] [76] [79] [83] reused from Chapters 1–10:

Chapter 12: Master Reference Index (continued)

References [9] [19] [23] [39] [40] [65] [77] [79] [80] reused from Chapters 1–11:

Appendix References

[83] BlueWallet & Phoenix. (2023). Self-Custody Lightning Wallets. https://bluewallet.io | https://phoenix.acinq.co
[84] Muun. (2023). Bitcoin and Lightning Wallet. https://www.muun.com
[85] Kaspersky. (2023). How to Store Cryptocurrency Safely: Hardware Wallets and Multisig Explained. https://www.kaspersky.com/blog/crypto-storage-security/47349/